SILLY

BIRDS

ARTWORK AND STORIES
BY
SHERRI JONES

THE REALITY OF
EVERY DAY IS A MIRACLE

A long time ago I started writing stories about some of the things that I have noticed or came upon. I call it (The Reality of Every Day is a Miracle). This book has some of the short stories from that book. It also has some short stories from my book (Bird's Big and Small). If we look at all of the things that go on in one day, we can find many blessings.

THE COMMUNICATION TREE

SILLY
BIRDS

CONTENTS

Silly Birds, 7

Back Porch Birds, 8

The Turkey Gang, 11

Geese, 12

Airplane Birds, 15

Cat Movie, 17

Hawk to the Rescue, 18

Heart Hawks, 18

Quails, 19

Bats, 23

Nest of Babies, 27

Big Bird Feast, 28

Mamma Bird, 29

Seagulls, 30

The Return of the Great White Bird, 31

Flapping Eagle, 37

Stuffed Eagle Buddy, 38

Combat Air Show, 39

Eagle Prayers, 40

Crows, 40

Hey Little Blue Bird, 42

I Saw an Eagle, 47

Born Free & Fly like an Eagle, 49

Beaver Creek, 51

Song Bird, 54

Woodpecker, 55

Dodo, 56

For New Thing to Grow, 58

SILLY
BIRDS

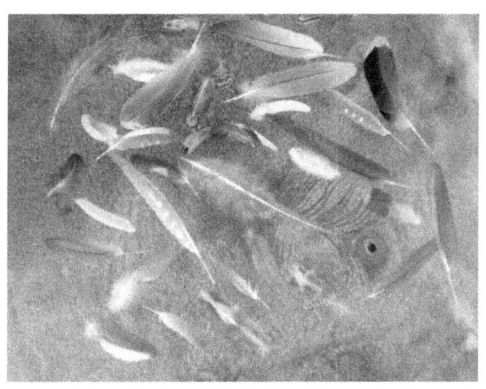

SILLY BIRDS

I have noticed over the past ten years, birds and animals that people hardly ever see, moving into town and hanging out at local parks and in people's yards. Not afraid of people and acting a little confused and minding their own business as if people do not exist. I remember when I was younger that animals and birds were used to the woods and fields. They stayed away from the cities, people and the smell of chemicals. I think they are getting used to noise and chemicals and that their homes are being destroyed. I see turkeys in an apartment complex, cranes walking around a community center, a duck on the top of a house, a rooster in a front yard. The list goes on. I think that they are being pushed out of their homes and maybe confused from chemicals. There are two marshes on the north side of town and the animals have been trickling out. They are nice to see but for health reasons it is sad for them. It is also not safe for children that might try to pet or feed them.

BACK PORCH BIRDS

Over twenty years ago. Just out of the blue I decided to put a bunch of bird feeders in my back yard and on my balcony patio. I would go outside and sit at the patio table to eat. It was nice to watch the ones who came and ate too. I had attracted many different kinds. I would not have imagined this. Many of them I was not familiar with or know what kind that they were. I enjoyed it very much.

This also may attract many little animals. I get squirrels and chipmunks. They are really cute little friends. Some of them can be very brave. They like to eat some of the seeds. Some times I give them unsalted nuts. Too much salt is not good for them.

One place that I lived at, most of the chipmunks in the neighborhood knew me. I called my morning time, breakfast with the chipmunks. I would go outside with my coffee and a bowl of nuts. Then would set the nuts down and they would just appear. I would sometimes get twenty to thirty of them. I did have one favorite. It was the first one. It came close to me one day. I told it to wait and went inside and got a bowl of nuts and put it down right next to it. Then I told it, "Now go tell all of your family and friends that they can come have breakfast here." I was just being silly talking to it and not serious. Then it took off and came back. Then all of the others showed up, they were there within a few minutes. I had about twenty of them. This one would sit about a half a foot away from me. After that it became a regular thing.

It is strange that when I see the birds and animals eat from my feeders I feel some kind of flattery. I know that they are only after the food. I guess it's just from their presence. Like their presence is a present for me. I thank the creator as in, "Oh I am flattered." And I like when they flutter and make me flutter too.

One night I decided to go outside and look at the stars and enjoy a beautiful night. I heard a noise of a small animal going underneath my chair. My assumption to the feel of the size of it, that it was one of my cats. I sat there enjoying the night for about fifteen minutes or so. I heard it move again then looked down and saw that it was a possum. I have no idea how I attracted that possum under my chair. It might have been after something in the garden next to me. It went off into the garden. Rarely does a person see a possum in the city of Madison. There were *no fields or woods by where I lived. I had also noticed that some twin baby skunks were hanging out in the yard around that same time period.*

It is possible that because I was feeding the birds, squirrels and chipmunks that they started to come to me. I believe that they were looking for food.

THE TURKEY GANG

In 2010 it was in the news that there was a gang of turkeys cruising suburban neighborhoods stalking, circling, chasing and attacking people, breaking into houses, tearing things up and stalking a school yard. One crashed through a closed window to get into a house. One went after a mail carrier and jumped into the mail truck. They were referred to as a gang with a leader. There was comments on the intelligence of them as to that the turkeys were plotting the attacks. There was an assumption to the idea that they may have been after whatever the particular people were wearing. They didn't try to attack everybody only certain people, mostly mail carriers. I do not know what became of it. This was not normal turkey behavior.

GEESE

While at a park in McFarland, Wisconsin around thirteen years ago, I saw geese with deformed beaks and feet. They were red and bubbled in different areas. I was curious as to what caused it. It was sad and it bothered me. My assumption was that it was probably from something toxic or maybe birth defects.

A few years later some of the ducks and geese were being moved out of some of the surrounding areas because they were eating toxins, leaving their feces by the way sides and polluting the water. I heard that they were bagged and removed.

I went to visit another park that was in Madison shortly before the ducks and geese were removed. I had been chased by the geese - one big one in particular. They wanted my bread bag. They were squawking and running. I was trying to run as fast as I could. I made it to my vehicle safely. A lot of people were experiencing that same thing. I loved feeding the ducks and geese with my kids when they were young and had never experienced that. I have had some run at me wanting food and squawking in the past, but not that aggressively. They appeared real mad and desperate. Geese have eyes on the side of their heads and don't see straight ahead very well. They all seemed to have gone crazy. I found out that the bread that people have been feeding them for years is bad for them. They need to eat more natural food in a cleaner environment. Now there are different geese and ducks in Madison, WI. Most of the old ones are gone. It seems a little mixed up. I don't see anywhere near as many mallards as I used to. It seems like a fad - out with the old and in with the new. It is sad and unnatural!

Shortly after my experience of being chased, I went into a local gas station. A man working there started talking to me about the geese at the park being crazy. I hadn't mentioned anything to him about what I had just experience. He said that he made a video for public access TV at the park showing the geese charging people. They used catsup for fake blood to make it look like the people were being attacked. He made a comedy horror movie. Then I went on to tell him of my experience. I was hoping that I wasn't one of the people shown running in the video. He told me that he would give me a copy of it. He said to meet him at the gas station at a certain time. He wasn't there and had no longer worked there.

It was something to see all of the people that would get out of their vehicles, scream and run when they saw the geese coming. They were real loud and could run real fast. It seemed like they had taken over the whole park. It's sad to see such nice calm animals acting all freaked out like that. It used to be one of my favorite things to do was to go visit those ducks and geese, even after my children were grown. I would go over there just to visit them.

Not being in the right environment and not eating the right food made them sick, hungry and crazy!

AIRPLANE BIRDS

During 2010 there had been problems here at the airports in Madison, WI. There were issues of ducks and geese causing problems with air flights by flying in the pathway of the airplanes. They were also hanging out at the airport on the runways and making messes. Some people wanted the state to just murder them all. Others were trying to look for solutions as to filling the food pantries and saving some of the economy. Talk was about the birds eating toxins, not being healthy and destroying the environment. Then it was kill them and feed them to the homeless or donate to the food pantries. This is revolting! Some were thinking of the bagging and moving idea again. They are scrambled and scattered, this is a sad situation. It makes me wonder what is wrong with peoples minds if they think that the birds are too toxic to have around, then want to feed them to people who are in poverty situations.

One of my sons came over one day to cook a duck that somebody had given him. He wanted to share the duck and cook for people. It was in a white package with black writing and no brand name on it. It looked to me like a commodity. I was afraid of it and nobody would eat it but him. He believed that it was store bought. What he left here ended up in the garbage and was wasted. We had a fear of where did it come from and was it clean of toxins. This is a shame!

CAT MOVIE

I found an educational bird video with a picture of a cardinal on the cover. I was seeing a lot of cardinals around that time. I was interested in learning about them. When I played it my cats started watching it and became excited. My cat Star charged at the TV and stopped real fast in the prowl pounce position. The other cat Medicine got close to the screen and watched with excitement. Some flute music stared playing in one of the scenes. Medicine started lightly pawing the birds on the screen in sync with the music. It looked like a synchronized dance with her paws. Like a cat ballet dance or an orchestra conductor. She was very graceful. I didn't care for the movie but they loved it.

Every once and a while I would yell, "Hey Medicine, I'm putting your movie in." She would run to the TV and wait with excitement. She would watch it from the beginning to the end every time with no distractions. It's about a 30 minute show. It *wasn't about just cardinals there were various birds.*

HAWK TO THE RESCUE

Eight years ago I had prayed for my friend's property. I asked the creator to protect her, some kids and the property. A couple of days later, she had an argument with a visitor in the same spot. A red-tailed hawk flew down and landed on his head, biffed him up a little bit, then flew off. I do not think that he was hurt but I bet it scared the heck out of him. She didn't know that I had said a prayer in that same spot. She was laughing because the hawk came and protected her. It was good timing.

HEART HAWKS

February 13 2012, I was outside standing under a tree. Two red-tailed hawks flew in my direction, they were side by side. When they were got close in front of me right above, they split up and both did a half circle going in the opposite direction from each other then disappeared. The pattern that they flew looked like the top shape of a heart. Right then I remembered that it was the day before Valentines Day.

QUAILS

My sister-in-law came over one day and said that her giant lizard had died and that she was thinking of putting another type of animal in the cage. She likes to amuse the grandchildren. The large cage takes up about a quarter of her living room. We got on the internet and were looking at pet ads. Meanwhile we were talking about all of the nice bird feathers that her and her fiancé had given me. We came across an ad for chickens and quails for sale. Well we thought, "My that's different." She called the man and we decided to go see them. She had planned on getting a couple of something. We were prepared with a couple of pet carrier.

When we arrived and got out of the vehicle, we could hear all kinds of bird noises coming out of a big barn shed. We questioned the man about the bird barn. He was very nice and gave us a tour. He had many different kinds of wild birds and chickens living in there. Some were injured that he was doctoring. Some were for sale chickens. He had many pigeons and white doves not caged, with perches for them. While giving us the bird tour he told us their stories.

The man had a whole lot of pigeons and doves living there. He said that he was breeding paticular breeds of them in the past but after they leave and go home with somebody they sometimes escape from the people and then return back to him. He pointed one out in paticular that had been retuning from other states. Other ones that were not his had joined in with them and took up residency. It flattered him so he just decided to keep feeding and sheltering them, they come and go as they please.

My sister-in-law went with him into a different barn to see the quails and took along the pet carriers. She returned to the car with a dozen little babies. She said that he told her that quail babies are very nice and rarely ever bite. She said that he had an unbelievable amount of quails. This was a huge quail farm. I became curious so he gave me a tour of the quail barn too. He showed me the incubators, babies, eggs and told me about their lifestyles. He had them all sectioned off in areas according to age. I was amazed as to how many quails that I was seeing. Seeing is believing as to how many quails that there were. I had never really ever thought very much about quails before. This was an amazing experience.

After returning home my sister-in-law said that she had been cooking the eggs and giving them away. She said that she had been complemented on the taste of them. The *thought of eating one myself did not amuse me. The idea that the people that she worked with and that others loved eating them did. I do not think that I could eat a quail or quail egg.*

When I went to visit her, I noticed that she had more quails then what I remember us picking up. She said that she loved having them so she went back to that farm and got another dozen. She said that she only had one real naughty bully one out of the whole bunch and a few that were a little naughty. She also said that the males are more aggressive then the females. She gave the bully one to her fiancé who has a whole room full of different exotic birds. He just put him in a separate cage.

Some of her friends became fond of the quails and wanted some for themselves for pets. So she stated giving them away and went and got more. I guess people love them once they find out about them because they are so very nice. They are a different kind of pet then what most people would think to have.

The man from the farm said that his farm has been becoming popular for the sales of the quails. They are inexpensive. My sister-in-law's purpose was to have nice tame pets and something interesting for the grandkids to look at.

The quail house in her living room is real cute and funny. They are real low maintenance pets. They are very innocent and cute little birds. She put clear plastic rodent tunnels and toys in the cage. The quails play and run around through the tunnels. I laughed when I saw them running through the tunnels. They are funny and entertaining. I would have never imagined this. They are cute goofy little birds!

BATS

My parents had some real pretty purple flowered vines that grew outside along the front of the house. It became the home of many fruit bats for many years. They never bothered me because I was used to them. They would sometimes fly around at nighttime when aroused. One of my older sisters didn't like them. They never bothered anybody that I know of as far as attacking goes. I know that one flew into somebody once. They seemed to be very peaceful and didn't harm anything. My dad just let them live there. I think that he tried to scare them away a few times because my mother and sister were irritated. They were persistent to have their home. He didn't believe in harming things, they weren't hurting anything. They just weren't very pretty and they gave some people the creeps. They liked to hide in the vines, hang upside down from the vine post and fly around at night.

I know it probably freaked out some visitors. Most people didn't notice it during the day. If people came to visit at night I had sometimes alerted them. "Just ignore the bats they won't hurt you." They would fly around real fast like a flash of something black and people would wonder what it was. Now as an adult I see how crazy it may have seemed. My father figured if something in nature was not hurting anything, then do not bother it.

When I saw what a bats body looked like in a book, they are like mice without the long tails, they have wings and fangs. They are not birds, they are mammals. They are the only mammals that can really fly like a bird. They liked to come out at night because that was when their food was easier to get. They can eat thousands of insects per day.

A lady I know from up north had a vampire bat fly on to the back of her neck, then it flew away. She had been bitten and was bleeding. She didn't know that it had bitten her until she saw it fly away. She had two bleeding puncture marks on her neck, it was real strange. The poor woman has probably had nightmares. She went to the doctor of course to make sure that she did not have some kind of strange infectious disease.

What is also strange is that it was daytime and she was in an open area.

It appeared that the bat singled her out. From what I have read about them is that they have been known for biting people but rarely. They prefer to attack animals. They bite, get some blood then fly off fast. The surrounding area was all woods with many animals. This is why I felt that it singled her out. They sleep during the day in dark places and hang by their feet. Most bats are not out in the open during the day. I had read that they have radar for warmth and that may be how it singled her out or sensed something about her blood.

I did not know that vampire bats really existed. I thought that they were just from TV shows and fabricated. The fruit bats that I knew outside my house growing up didn't bite anybody. I do not think that the vampire bat was normally from that area. People were freaking out when they heard about it. It seemed like something out of a creepy movie.

Bats have wings, so I decided to add some bat stories to the bird stories.

NEST OF BABIES

I was with a friend at a place in the woods. There was a small shed on the property. We were working doing things preparing to build something. I heard tiny little chirp sounds and looked and saw a little nest full of baby birds. It was sitting on a ledge outside of the shed. My friend's little dog started barking at them and trying to jump up at it. It was way too high up for the little dog to get at.

A couple of hours later I asked my friend if he saw the baby birds and he said no. He went and looked and said that there was no nest. I told him, "Yes just look." I went to point it out to him and saw that it was gone. We looked on the ground and there was no sight of it anywhere. We didn't think it would be possible for the little dog to get it down. It is possible that with the sight of us and the little dog that the mom moved the nest.

I questioned this to others and had been informed that some little birds are very strong and have been known for moving their nest when in danger. It was unimaginable to me that a tiny little bird would have that strength. Amazing!

THE BIG BIRD FEAST

I was in the grocery store one day and I saw something fly across the ceiling real fast. Other people in the store saw it too. I said, "What was that a bat?" It was moving so fast that they could not tell either. We saw it again and noticed that there was more then one of them. I was approaching the pet food isle. When I started to turn into the isle, little tiny birds flew away from the bird seed area. I looked at the bags of bird seed and a bunch of them were ripped open. Oh the different *varieties of food, what a feast. They were getting in through the ceiling tiles and feasting.*

While writing this bird story, I heard somebody on the TV say "That is a big bird." I turned around to look and saw that it was just a lady showing off her platter, with a large turkey on it. I had just named this story The Big Bird Feast, then turned around and saw a different kind of big bird feast on the television.

MOMMA BIRD

When my children where young, I would tell them that I was the momma bird and that they were the baby birds. That momma birds always protect their baby birds. Momma bird never allows anybody to hurt her babies.

I had issues with two of my sons that were being stalked by bullies and one who would beat up the ones that picked on his brothers. So the issue was to teach the two to defend themselves and to teach the other to defend and only fight when needed. They were nice and didn't like to fight. I decided that something needed to be done about the situation. I was a martial artist and decided to enroll them all in a martial arts school.

The purpose of martial arts is self defense and fighting only if necessary. They were very physically flexible and used protective sparring gear. So it became fun and natural for them. They all liked a big eagle patch so they all had eagle patches on the back of their uniforms. They all became champions and won almost every karate tournament. This was how this momma bird protected her baby birds.

SEAGULLS

In the past I have had a fear of seagulls, when they screamed. I was talking to someone about how I didn't like when they screamed. They and their feathers would give me the creeps. A couple days after talking about it, I was at a park and a bunch of them were flying around. My Sister threw some food in the air. They flew by and caught the food in the air, right above her. So I started throwing food in the air too. It was real neat because they would fly as low as five feet above our heads and catch the food. They were floating above our heads. After that I wasn't afraid of them anymore. I found that I liked them very much.

THE RETURN OF THE GREAT WHITE BIRD

One day I could hear what had sounded like an eagle whistle and it was very loud. My granddaughter and a neighbor and I had seen a golden eagle out here about a month before this and I was hoping that it had returned. We hear hawks out here all of *the time during the summer. I felt drawn to the sound of this bird and the need to go find it. I knew it was real close but could not see it. I followed the whistling to a tree. I looked and didn't see it anywhere. After a few minutes it flew out of the tree above me and it was a huge white bird with maybe 4 to 6 darker colored under wing feathers. I saw the back and under body but not the face. It was shaped like an eagle and flew and sounded like one. My automatic thought was that I was seeing a white eagle. It did a circle then disappeared into the sky and blended in with the white clouds. I watched for a couple of minutes for it to come back.*

I called a friend and he came over right away and we waited a little bit to see if it would come back. It was nowhere in sight. All we saw were hawks. When I called him, he just happened to be about a half a mile away on the same hwy in the direction that the bird flew. He lives in the next town over in the other direction.

When he was driving away a little red cardinal flew past his windshield. It was funny because, in the past I had told his wife that whenever I go to an event that they put on, about world peace. A red cardinal flies past my windshield while driving to it. I told him to tell her about it. I had commented about the cardinals to her in the past. Then found out that she has a big thing for red cardinals. I have read that cardinals are associated with the good energy of the sun. I know that it was a very special day of blessings.

I decided to stake out the big white bird. I got some food for it and got up early in the morning and sat out by that tree for hours waiting its return. Neighbors had said that they had seen it often. They said that it was a light colored large hawk. A few days later I saw a large light colored blondish white hawk with a few dark colored feathers. I believe it to be the one that they were seeing. The bird that I had seen was more white and bigger. I finally gave up after a few days.

I felt that the creator had given me a miracle to witness. It was so exciting that it made me cry in a good way. White and albino or black things are considered very holy to many cultures around the world.

I started an investigation on white eagle and hawk sightings. I found that sightings had been made of very large partial albino female red tail hawks. A few had been sighted over the past decade. I could only find one sighting in WI. Most of them were all white with a little red on the tip of the tails. The bird that I saw had a white tail. I believed that it was an eagle. Without seeing the head, I could not say for sure what it was, just a beautiful big white bird that blended and disappeared like magic in with the clouds.

During the time that I was staking it out. I had been sitting outside baiting it waiting and hoping that it would return with the camera ready. I went inside for a few minutes. One of my sons who was visiting *had seen it when he left. I was inside and had missed it. He was able to look at it real good. It was sitting on a pole next to that tree and looking at him as he got into his vehicle, then flew away. It was a very big albino hawk that was the size of an eagle and sounded like an eagle. He didn't tell me until right after New Years. He thought that I was out with it and watching it. It had returned and I missed it.*

He and I have witnessed many rare holy bird experiences together. That was why he thought that I was just hanging out with it. I remember in the past him talking about having dreams of a white eagle. In my mind it was some kind of hawk eagle.

It came back a few times at the beginning of this summer. A neighbor had seen it and confirmed it also as an extremely large albino hawk. It tried to pick up his little dog. My son was also had his little dog with him when he saw it. He was carrying his.

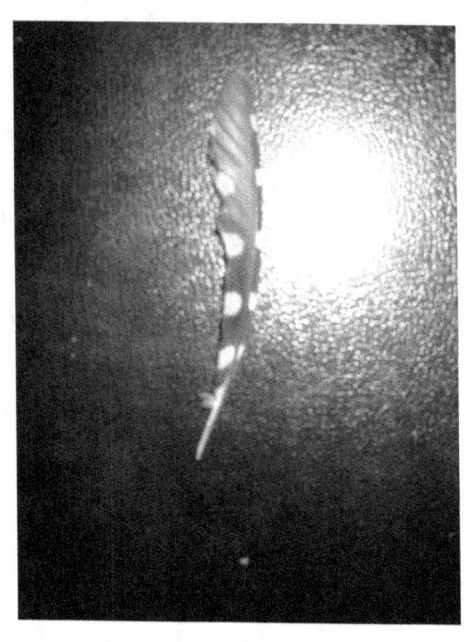

During the time that I was waiting its return, I had found a little black and white polka - dot feather. I had also seen a picture of a friend that I had not seen for a very long time wearing a shirt just like the feather. I gave him the feather. He is a Native American drummer and it was a woodpecker feather. Within many Native American cultures woodpeckers are in relation to the drum. He is Ojibwe!

FLAPPING EAGLE

I was at a Festival a few years ago. Some people were taking pictures of people with eagles. They stand behind the person and hold the eagle's feet then take the picture. It looks like the eagle is standing with the person or on their shoulder. I thought that it was cute so I decided to try it. When I got into place and he put the eagle up behind me. The eagle kept flapping her wings and the man was having a hard time keeping her still. It was kind of scary but real cool. She was flapping her wings behind my back and trying to fly. I didn't know if she wanted to jump on me and attack or if she liked me and was excited. It was a neat feeling having those wings flap right behind my back. I ran once then went back then almost ran again. The man got her to settle down and then took the picture.

I didn't see her doing that with other people who were getting their pictures taken. I have no idea why that eagle acted that way or what her plan was. She may have just wanted to fly away or land on my shoulder. The thought of one of those big claws on the shoulder was kind of scary. Maybe she didn't want her picture taken. I love humor! And love the fact that it was a she.

STUFFED EAGLE BUDDY

While visiting a friend she showed me her guest room, there was a stuffed eagle toy on the bed. I was kidding and said, "Oh I get to sleep with that stuffed eagle." I put it to the side of the bed when I went to sleep and woke up with it in my arms. I thought that she put it there and she didn't. I am used to sleeping with a pillow like that. I must have grabbed it in my sleep as if it were my pillow. It was real funny and cute!

COMBAT AIR SHOW

I was talking to one of my cousins on the phone one day. We were talking about eagles. I told him to pray to the eagles with tobacco and he would be blessed. He said that he didn't think that anything would happen. The following day I received an email from him saying that he had seen the best combat air show ever. An osprey caught a fish and two eagles went after it. He said that it was some of the best maneuvers that he had ever seen.

A couple of days after that he saw an eagle at a park. At that particular time he was doing some of our family history study of the land before and after the whites had moved into Cherokee, Chota, Tanasi (Monroe and Loudon Counties of Tennessee.) He was studying the areas of where and when it was taken over and the Natives were pushed out across the River at Fort Loudon (Little Tennessee River) Then The Trail of Tears, the flooding of the land that was caused by a dam that was built, after the Cherokee removal, causing some of the homeland to be under water.

While he was working on the history he had found out that nobody was taking care of our family cemetery. He decided to help the family and cleaned it up. During that time he had been seeing eagles.

EAGLE PRAYERS

I have seen many miraculous things with bald eagles. An elder told me that when I am scared and confused to pray to the eagles. He said that the eagles will guide me.

CROWS

I love to watch crows walk, they look like they have an arrogant attitude. Like the way some people walk when they are trying to be the boss and look cool. They walk like they have no fear, are in charge and tough. I think that they are funny to watch. They have an I am cool attitude that makes me laugh. When a big group of them are in a tree talking at the same time, they can make a whole lot of noise. They all sound like they are bickering and complaining. I remember when I was young my mother would call people who complain, crows. Ravens are real noisy too! A whole lot of ravens and crows can really stir up a whole lot of ruckus of noise in the woods.

Some people are afraid of Crows and Ravens and call them witch birds. I like them and think that they sometimes like to show people things. They make noise to get the attention of a person. When the person goes to looks at what it was squawking at. They sometimes find things and wonder how it got there.

HEY LITTLE BLUE BIRD

I was talking to my friend Dennis on the telephone one day. I told him that I was writing books about my bird experiences. I had mentioned A little pretty bird that was blue. He said that he wrote a bird song for a CD then he sang it to me. He said that he was in Sedona, Arizona way high up on a hill praying and was visited by hundreds of little birds that were blue. He wrote a story and song about it. He writes and sings Native story song's for children. He said that this song was gifted to him by the spirit of those birds in Sedona, Arizona. He mailed a CD of the song to me.

A few weeks after one of my sons came over with a little baby light blue parrot as a gift to me. I loved the parrot so my granddaughter and I started to sing Dennis's song to her. She was a smart little bird. The little bird watched me collect her feathers from the bottom of the cage and put them in clear bag.

One day I walked passed her and she made a loud noise. I turned around and she had a feather in her beak while looking at me, then she put her beak out side of the cage. I put my hand out and she placed the feather in my hand. She did the same thing the next day. She watched me make some earring out of them. She always seemed interested in watching me do things.

She was a whole lot of fun and real cute. She could find ways to escape and I was afraid that she would fly away. WI is not a good place for a tropical bird. She got outside one time and was hopping around the yard. I took her cage out and she got into it. I was glad that she didn't fly into the trees in the woods out here. She had a thing about the telephone speaker. She associated it with conversations and would start making very loud noises at certain people that I was talking too. She also liked to be hand fed. She appreciated having food given to her.

Sometimes she would surprise me and

make a tone or tunes that I had just done. She was still a baby and liked to practice her vocals. She could get pretty loud and feisty sometimes. What was funny is that she was not afraid of my Labrador or cat. She bit both of them right away. Neither the dog nor cat tried to hurt her at all. She realized that they liked her. Then they all became a cute little family of friends. They could walk around on the ground together and visit.

My granddaughter was six years old. She had just became attracted to Dennis's song and started singing it frequently. The bird was a parrot not a bluebird but a bird that was blue. The blue bird is a type of bird.

HEY LITTLE BLUE BIRD

Hey little blue bird in the sky
Why don't you come and just fly by
Hey little blue bird sitting in a tree
Why don't you come and sing a song
for me.
Hey little blue bird don't you know
Singing and playing way to go
Hey little blue bird in the sky
Why don't you come and sit right by
Hey little blue bird don't you know
Come and share your spirit way to go
Hey little blue bird, hey little blue bird,
Hey little blue bird, hey little blue bird
Hey little blue bird in the sky
Why don't you come and just say hi
Hey little blue bird in the sky
Why don't you come and sit right by
In the cedar and the sage
Singing the song to pass the day
Hey little blue bird, hey little blue bird
Hey little blue bird, hey little blue bird
Hey little blue bird, hey little blue bird,
hey little blue bird.
By Dennis Dillard (White Bear)

I SAW AN EAGLE

My granddaughter Brooklyn and I were walking in the woods. A big golden eagle flew out of a tree. She made up a song about it. A few days later I was telling a neighbor lady about it. She is almost 90 years old. She said that around that same time a big golden eagle landed in the yard that we share. It was staring at her while facing her big picture window. It opened it wings and started flapping them while looking at her through the window. She spoke about this with excitement. We had wondered if it was the same eagle and if that was where it went. Brooklyn sang the song to her.

She is one of the nicest and friendliest elder women I have ever met. Many children in the neighborhood enjoy her kindness. When she sees them, she always smiles and tells them what good kids they are. She has a way about her that just sparkles when she speaks. I believe that the eagle was a message from the creator letting her know that she is blessed. Eagles and hawks like to make whistling sounds. We hear the hawks outside whistling almost every day.

I SAW AN EAGLE

I saw an eagle flying from a tree.
I saw an eagle flying to the east.
I came with grandma
and a dog named Honey Bun.
We went up the hill
and down the hill again.
We searched every where for it
and it was gone.
My grandma and I put tobacco out.

By: Brooklyn Barbra Kast, Created
4/1/11

BORN FREE
AND
FLY LIKE AN EAGLE

As a kid I was trained to be a professional skater. I could roller skate and ice skate. I used to say that it was flying like an eagle. One of my favorite songs when I was a kid was Born Free. I made a skating routine with it when I was 12 or 13 years old. Only the music without the words could be used for the routine. The words were in my mind while doing the routine. As a kid I thought a lot about freedom, flying in the air, gliding and landing, turning and moving, with the arms stretched out in perfect place. Just like a bird and landing that perfect jump. Spinning fast and stopping fast, being able to move fast in small areas and weaving. That was my freedom as a child and loved every bit of it. Although this song was a movie theme about a big lion named Elsa. The words (born free) have a lot of meaning for a lot of different things.

BORN FREE

Born free as free as the wind blows
As free as the grass grows.
Born free to follow your heart.
Live free and beauty surrounds you.
The world still astounds each time
you look at a star.
Stay free where no wall divides you.
You're free as the roaring tide.
So there's no need to hide.
Born free and life is worth living.
But only worth living because you're
born free.

The thought of being free like an eagle and being in the way of the eagles. The thought is to think like the eagle without ego. We all have our own dreams and challenges in life.

Born Free was a movie from 1966 Columbia Pictures. It was based on a non - fiction book written by Joy Adamson in 1960. Song lyrics by Don Black and composed by John Berry. The song was sung by Matt Monro then made famous by Andy Williams. It was also done instrumental by Roger Williams. It won numerous awards.

BEAVER CREEK

One day I climbed down High Cliff Bluff to the bottom. I sat down on the grass by Beaver Creek My son climbed the stone wall to look in the small caves. I was praying and looking at the water; it was relaxing and felt real good. I was feeling a strong sense of peace. The water was pretty, it was real dark, looked black and it felt peaceful. I closed my eyes for a minute while praying and when I opened my eyes and turned my head a bird appeared. It was brown, chubby and around 10-12 inches in height. It was about two feet away from my face and looking at me. It was talking to me while flapping its wings and stayed in one spot floating, twinkling and fluttering. It was there for about two minutes then it vanished. It was very cute and it seemed very friendly.

The bird seemed like it was giving me a message. I called to my son and asked him if he saw the bird. He didn't see it. I knew that I was not dreaming.

I questioned one of my sisters later about what kind of birds were in that area. I believe that it was a sandpiper. They can fly up and down in a straight line real fast in a flash, zig-zag and stop in mid air. If it was a sandpiper it may have flown straight down then up or vice versa. I did not see the bird fly to me or away, it just appeared, spoke and then vanished. It may have also been on the ground and popped up when I turned around. Sandpipers stay on the ground a lot. They live around the water and wooded areas. There are a lot of American Woodcocks in that area. The woodcocks are a different color than the bird that I saw. They are in the same bird family of the brown sandpipers. They have been declining in population. I do not know for sure what kind of bird it was. The bird was a mystery.

After doing a history of the land I had found out that I was not the only person who had these types of experiences. I read accounts of birds that spoke to paticular people. Most birds in other places do not approach people like that.

I started to have strange memories and thoughts about people joking when they say something about somebody. If the person did not know how they knew. The person would say, "How did you know that?" and the replay would be, "A little birdie told me."

I am not real educated on birds or the science of them. I guess I think more in the ways of things that are of nature as being good. All animals and birds have their own personalities. They are individual within their species. I also think that the creator (God) wants us to be happy! When we seek happiness then things happen. These little good experiences make the balance.

SONGBIRD

Within the Cherokee culture there is a bird called the songbird. It comes to people to tell a story and takes the peoples stories as a messenger. Many other birds are known as messengers. Pigeons were used in the past for carrying and delivering letters to people. Doves are known for carrying the message of love and peace. When I think of a dove I think of elegance and grace. When seeing a songbird I see perfect balance and grace.

There are many stories in the Cherokee culture about the little chickadees. The chickadee, tsigilili, chickee, is a songbird. They are known to represent truth within telling a story as to reminding a person to focus. They are known for being messengers of truth.

WOODPECKER

It is said that the woodpecker is a drummer beating to its own drum with nature and mother earth with its own pattern and freedom. They wake people up to the truth and grounding for balance with the earth and clarity.

The woodpecker was famous within many Native American tribes for pecking holes in a branch from a tree which made a flute. They are known for bringing the flute to the many Native people. The flute has been used for many different reasons. One of the biggest purpose is to summon a loved one or for courtship. They have become very popular. Many people feel a very positive spiritual nature with playing and listening to them. They have many good spiritual purposes.

DODO

The dodo bird is an extinct flightless bird from the island of Mauritius. It became extinct sometime around 1660. They were big funny looking birds that stood around three feet or so tall and weighed 22 – 40 pounds. The males were bigger then the females. They had very short wings in size to their bodies. It is thought by some scientist that they couldn't fly because they ate a lot and over years their bodies change in proportion to their wings. They did not have very many predator animals on the island and food of fruit and nuts were abundant.

When sailors and visitors came to the land they used the dodo for food. It was said that the big goofy looking bird was not of very good taste, greasy and hard to chew. The dodo was known for being very friendly. They would walk up to people and befriend them. They were not hard to hunt, it is sad. It was a nice bird considered not very smart by some for being friendly to people.

The birds were named by some different nationalities. The Dutch word dodoor, sluggard dodarr. Portuguese, dodour, fool, crazy. They were said to have been very clumsy with big beaks as long as nine inches. It is believed that they went out of extinction from being eaten by visitors of the island.

The words were spelled differently, dodo, dodou, dodaar, dodoi, dodour, doo doo. So as of today the word is used to tease as in, dumb dodo, dodo bird, doi and doo. So if somebody makes a mistake they might say something like, doi or doo, silly dodo, as in not very smart or clumsy. So if you didn't know this before, now you do.

If they would have been able to fly or would not been so friendly, they might have survived extinction. Most birds of today will bite, peck or fly away. It is important for children to not approach birds and try to pet them. Some also might attack if a nest of babies is near. They are nice to watch, but it is best not to touch or hand feed them. If feeding them it is wise to give them healthy food by placing it then moving away to watch them eat. Some might also bite by mistake while feeding.

The ones that we see are here because they have survived extinction. Most of the birds that are going extinct are mostly being filled with toxins from the environment.

FOR NEW THINGS TO GROW

Many birds drop seeds out of their beaks while flying. Many of the seeds hit the soil then take root and things grow from those seeds.

Females and the earth both give birth, without them there would not be men, children or anything that grows. If we do not take care of the earth everything that grows will be destroyed. The earth has a heartbeat without that heartbeat we would not be here. There has to be a balance to stay afloat and we have to stay grounded to the earth in balance. That is why we say that the drum is a heartbeat of mother earth. We all need to keep the water clean too, so that we can keep our bodies, brains, food and the earth clean. It is common sense.

Children need to learn how to care for one another and the earth. We need to teach them about humanity, kindness and gentleness within their own nature. One of the main things to learn is that we are all equal within creation, discrimination is a sin.

They need to know how to care for the birds, animal and the earth. The future is upon them. We need to teach it as a responsibility with love and respect.

Within a mind of innocence, a child is powerful enough to retain the memory of knowing love power and the reality of it. This is why it is important to remember the innocence of children and to teach them well. I very much appreciate being taught this as a child.

I have written these stories in deep respect to all. For the people who appreciate their love of being a part of this earth our mother and the tree of life, the grandchildren, the trees that grow and sprout roots, branches and leaves of love for generations to come. In hopes of a good future for all living things as we grow on our life's path on to other generations.

SHERRI JONES

About The Author

I am an Interfaith Minister, a preacher of equal rights. I am culturally mixed by heritage (Irish, Native American, English, Scottish, Spanish, French and?) My Father's Mother was Native American and most of my beliefs are Native. I believe in freedom of speech and freedom of religious rights, freedom from all forms of discrimination (race, religion, culture, disability, diversity, age and gender.) We are all one on this earth our mother and we are all created equal.

May the Creator Bless You!

Sherri Jones

MUSICL BIRDS

Co Authors

Brooklyn Kast

&

Dennis Dillard

Thank you for your songs!

Understanding
cultrual
differences
is knowing
that
we are all
one.

THE END